TCHAIKOVSKY'S

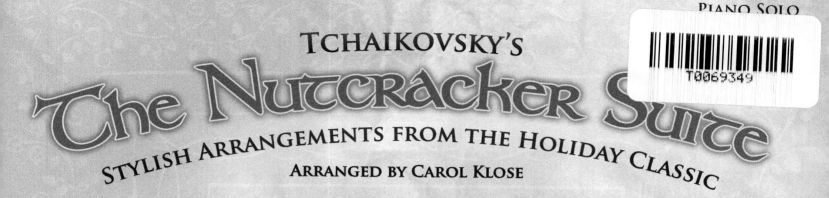

The Nutcracker Suite

STYLISH ARRANGEMENTS FROM THE HOLIDAY CLASSIC

ARRANGED BY CAROL KLOSE

ISBN-13: 978-1-4234-3167-1

HAL•LEONARD®
CORPORATION

7777 W. BLUEMOUND RD. P.O. BOX 13819 MILWAUKEE, WI 53213

In Australia Contact:
Hal Leonard Australia Pty. Ltd.
4 Lentara Court
Cheltenham, Victoria, 3192 Australia
Email: ausadmin@halleonard.com

Visit Hal Leonard Online at
www.halleonard.com

Tchaikovsky's *The Nutcracker Suite*

contains some of the most popular and beloved Christmas music of all time. Since its inception in the 1890s, both the ballet and the concert suite have been performed around the world. These special arrangements for piano solo are accessible to pianists of varying abilities, and retain all the magic and charm of the orchestrated version. The collection remains in the same sequence as the concert suite.

CONTENTS

OVERTURE

Pyotr Il'yich Tchaikovsky
Op. 71a

Sprightly

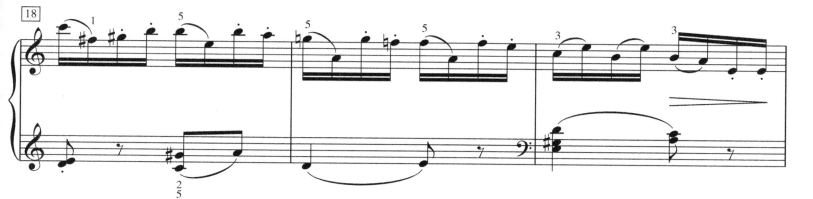

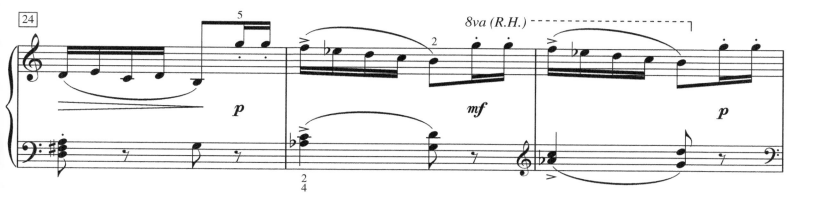

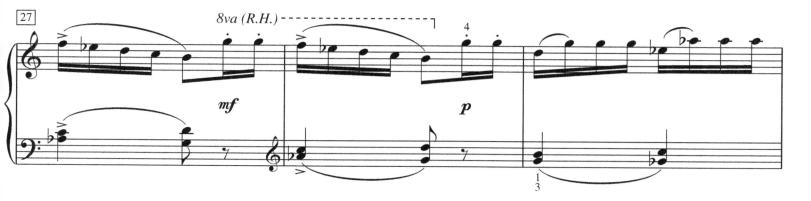

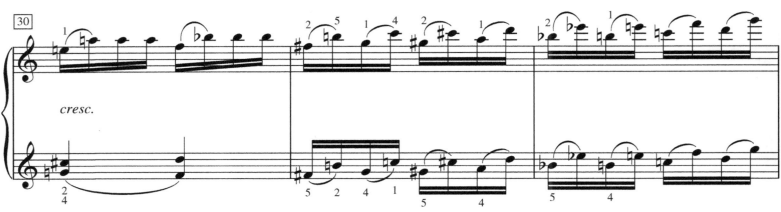

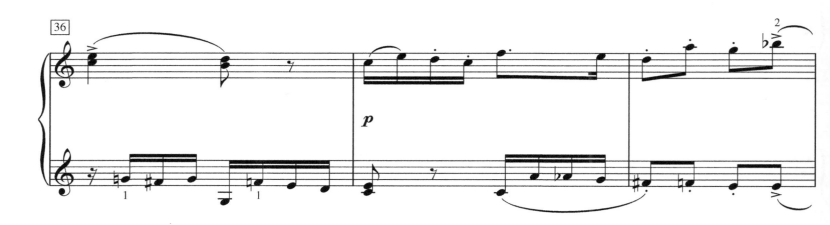

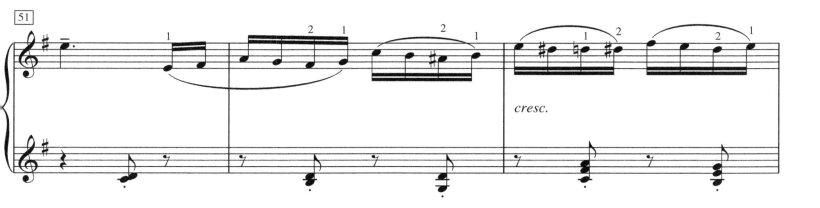

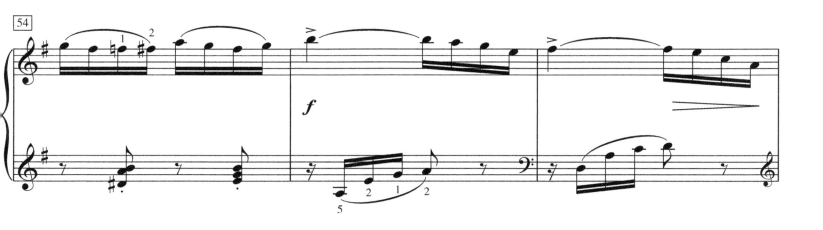

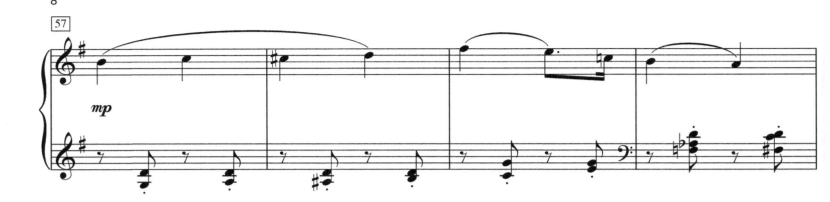

MARCH

Pyotr Il'yich Tchaikovsky

Brisk March tempo

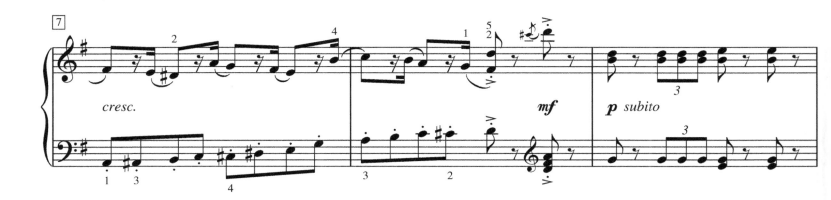

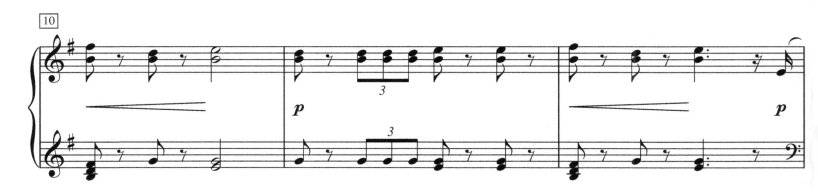

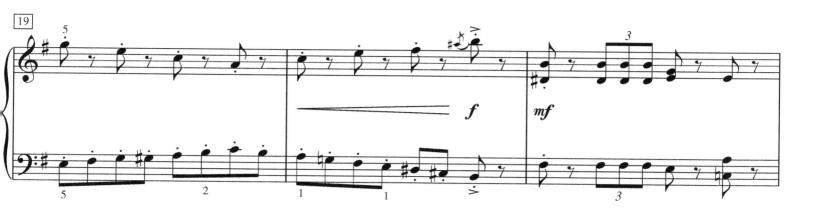

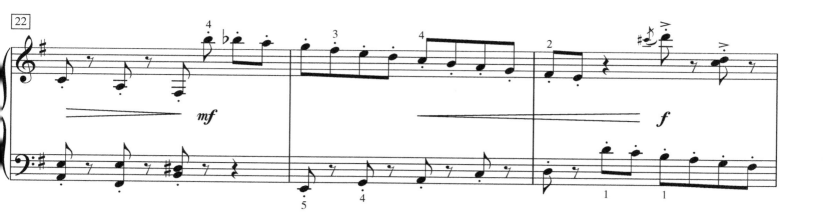

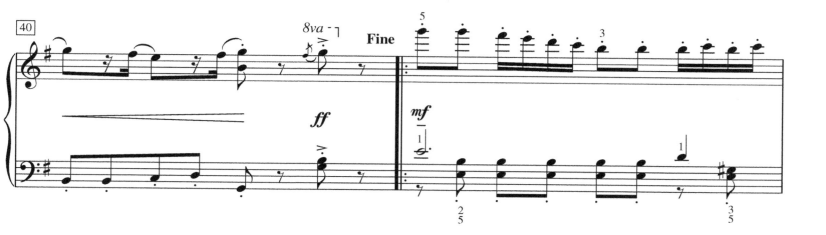

DANCE OF THE SUGAR PLUM FAIRY

Pyotr Il'yich Tchaikovsky

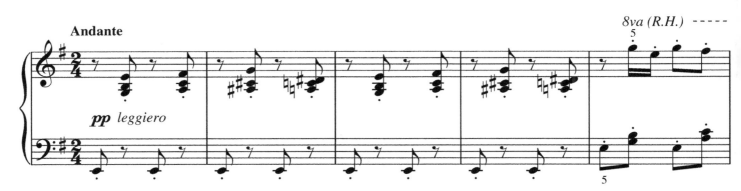

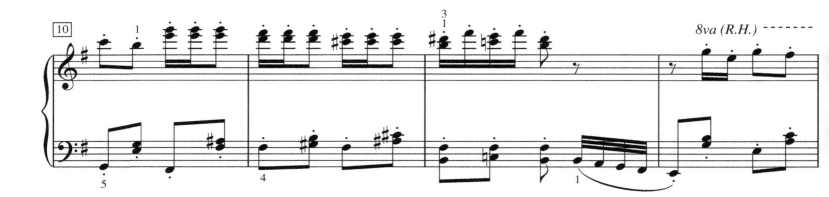

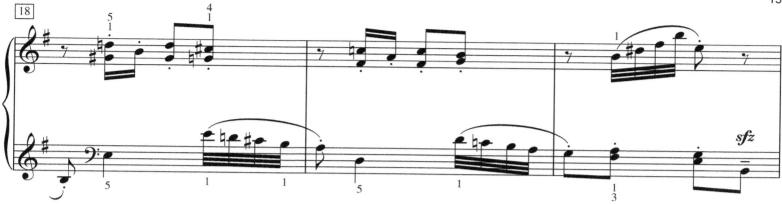

(L.H. over R.H.)

(L.H. over R.H.)

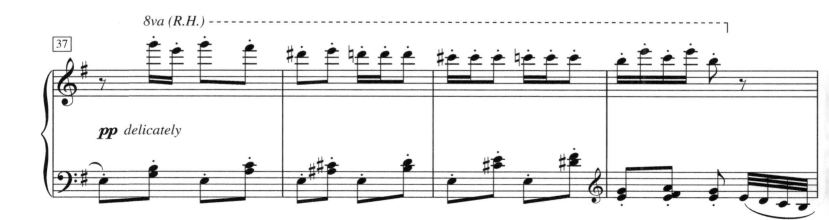

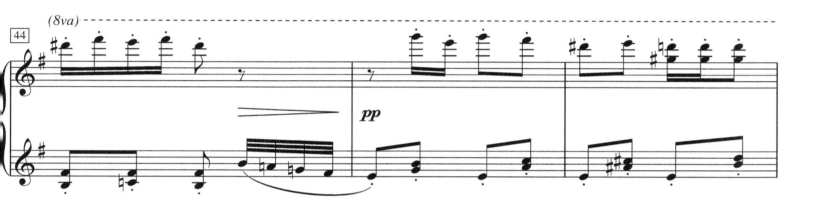

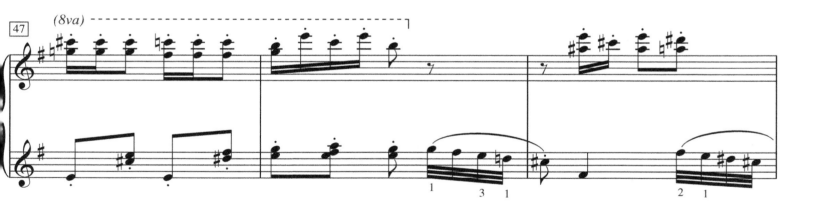

RUSSIAN DANCE
"Trepak"

Pyotr Il'yich Tchaikovsky

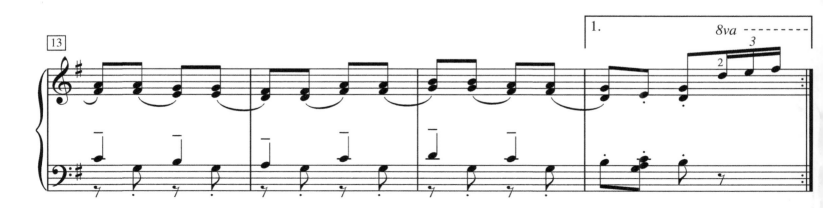

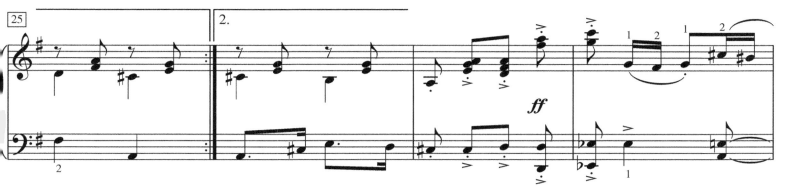

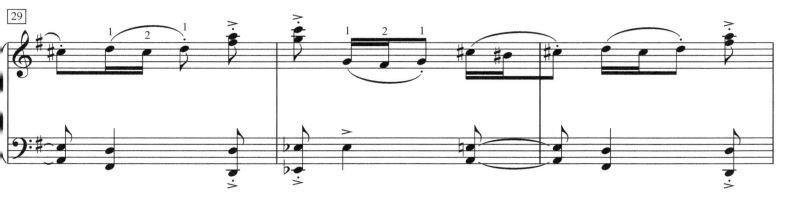

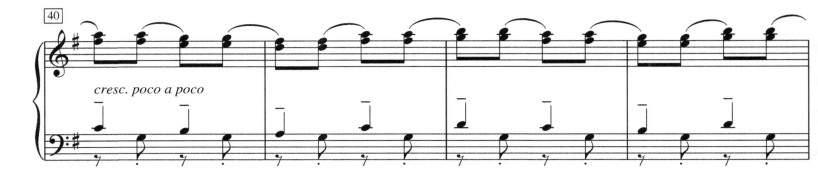

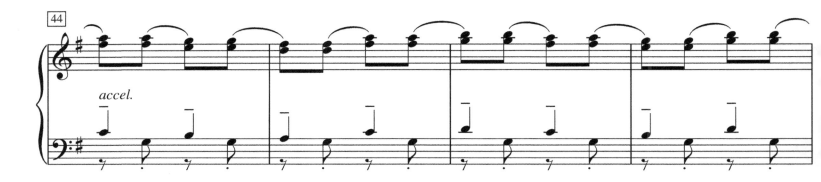

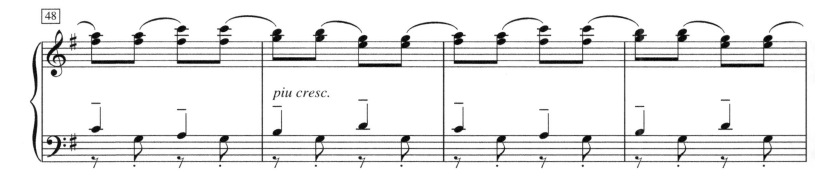

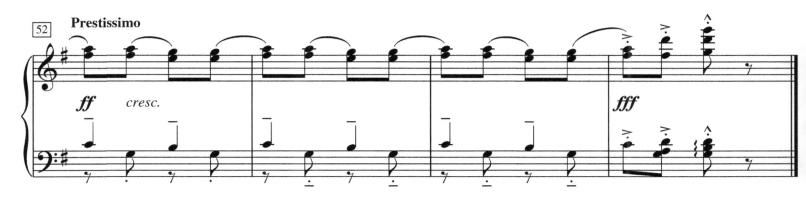

ARABIAN DANCE
"Coffee"

Pyotr Il'yich Tchaikovsky

Allegretto

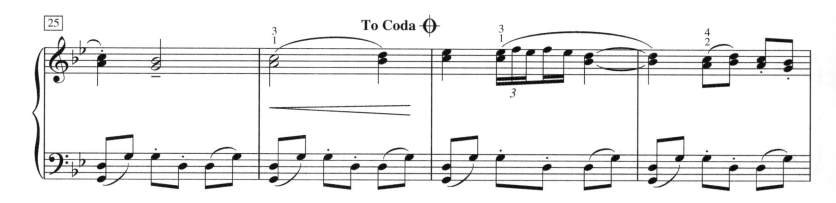

D.S. al Coda

CODA

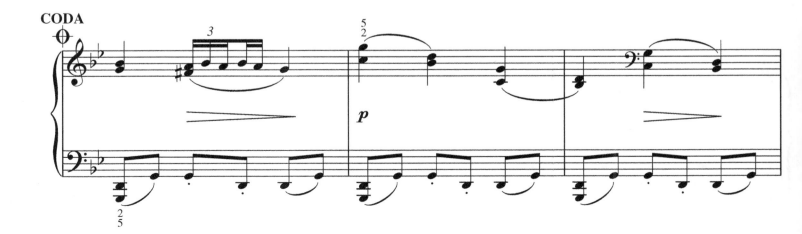

CHINESE DANCE
"Tea"

Pyotr Il'yich Tchaikovsky

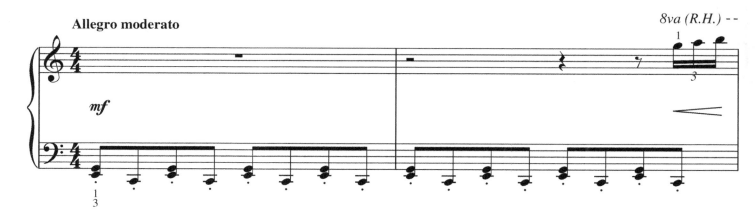

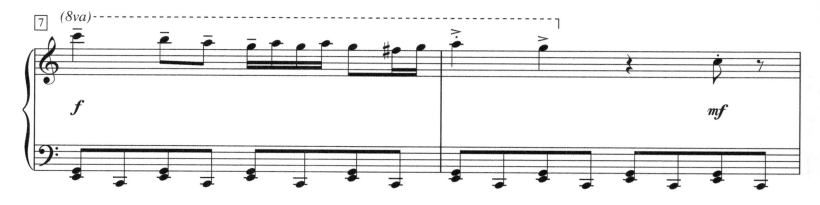

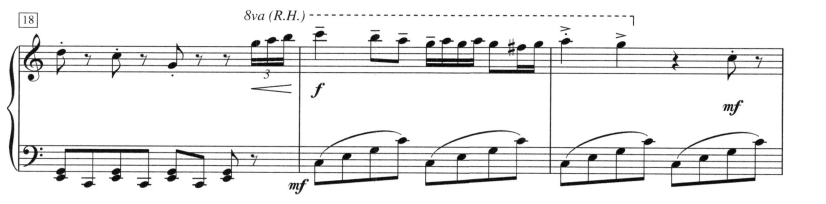

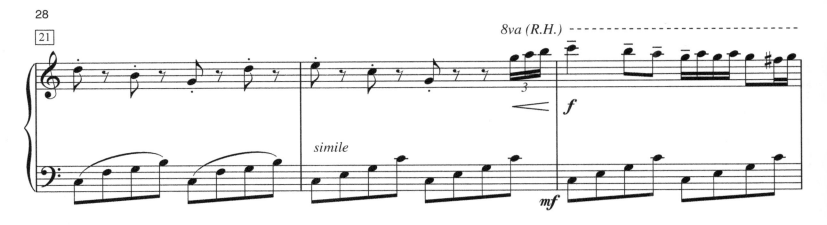

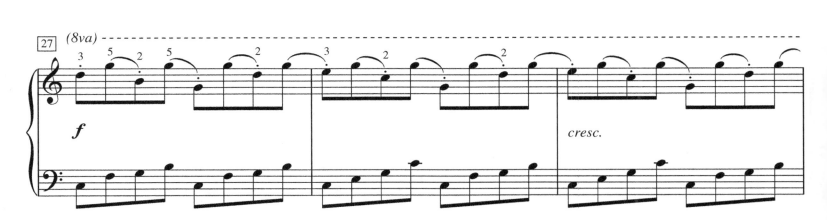

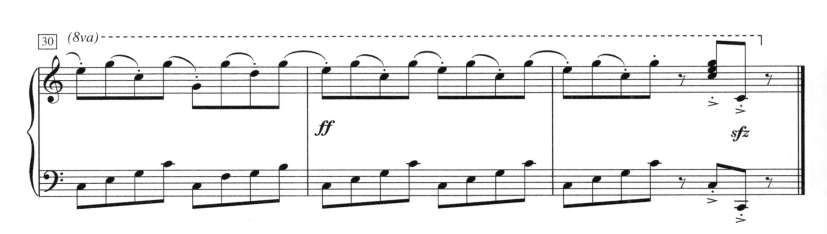

DANCE OF THE REED-FLUTES

Pyotr Il'yich Tchaikovsky

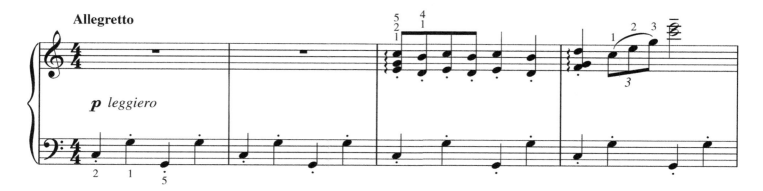

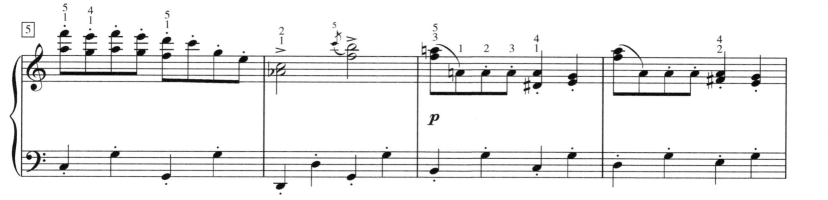

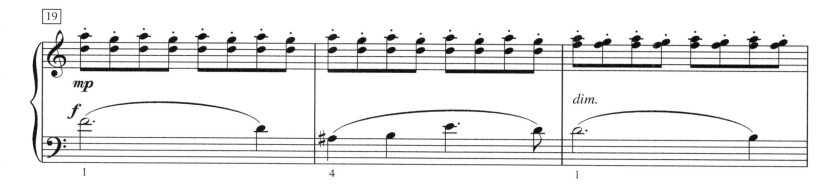

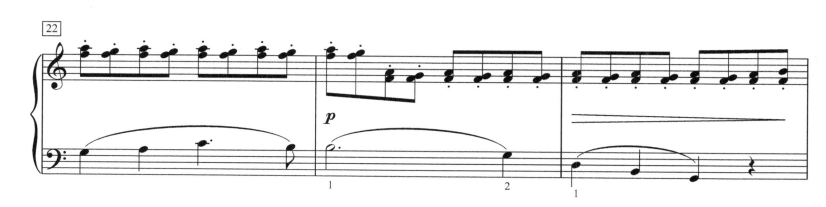

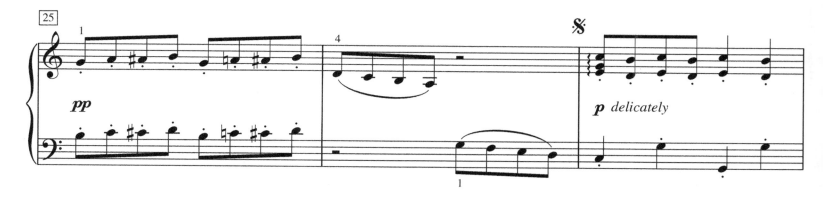

D.S. al Fine

WALTZ OF THE FLOWERS

Pyotr Il'yich Tchaikovsky

Moderate Waltz tempo

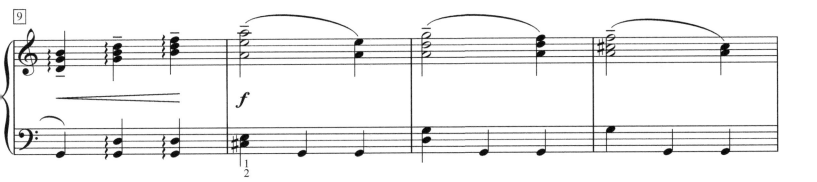

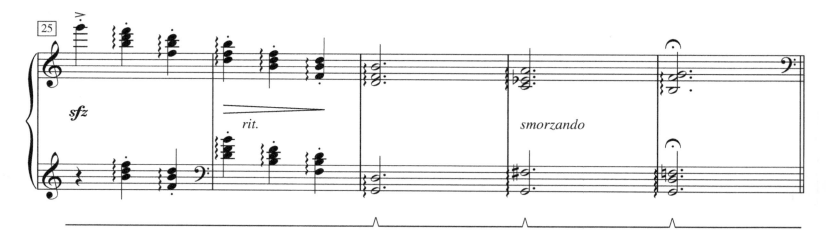

To Coda $\oplus$

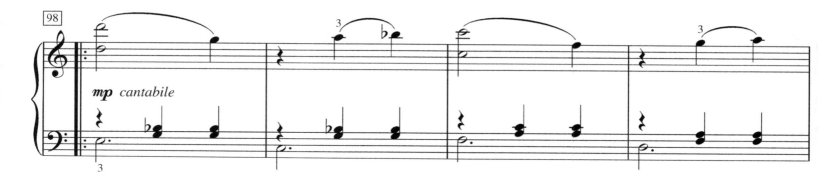

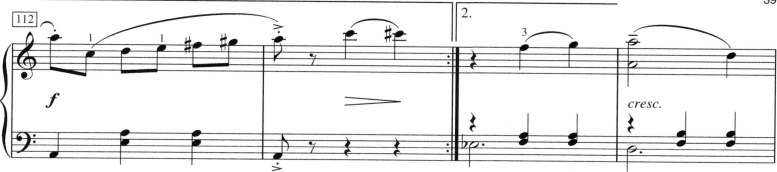

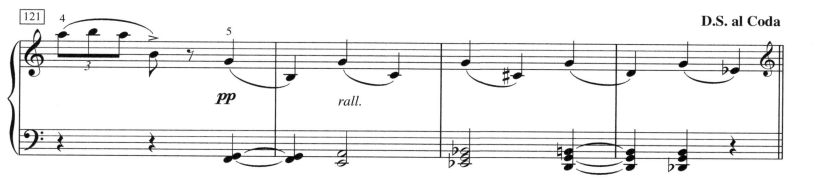

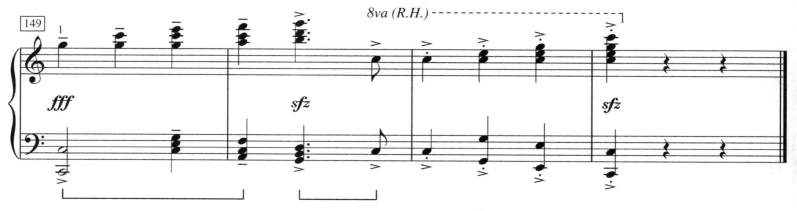